GREAT AMERICAN HORSES

AN IMAGINATION LIBRARY SERIES

MUSTANGS

America's Wild Horses

Best wishes — Victor Gentle

by Victor Gentle and Janet Perry

Gareth Stevens Publishing
MILWAUKEE

For a free color catalog describing Gareth Stevens' list of high-quality books and multimedia programs, call 1-800-542-2595 (USA) or 1-800-461-9120 (Canada).
Gareth Stevens Publishing's Fax: (414) 225-0377.
See our catalog, too, on the World Wide Web: gsinc.com

Library of Congress Cataloging-in-Publication Data

Gentle, Victor.
  Mustangs: America's wild horses / by Victor Gentle and Janet Perry.
    p. cm. — (Great American horses: an imagination library series)
  Includes bibliographical references (p. 23) and index.
  Summary: Describes the history and characteristics of the wild horses known as mustangs, as well as efforts to keep them from disappearing.
  ISBN 0-8368-2131-9 (lib. bdg.)
  1. Mustang—Juvenile literature. 2. Wild horses—Juvenile literature. [1. Mustang. 2. Wild horses. 3. Horses.] I. Perry, Janet, 1960- . II. Title. III. Series: Gentle, Victor. Great American horses.
  SF293.M9G45   1998
  636.1'3—dc21   98-14792

First published in 1998 by
Gareth Stevens Publishing
1555 North RiverCenter Drive, Suite 201
Milwaukee, WI 53212 USA

Text: Victor Gentle and Janet Perry
Page layout: Victor Gentle, Janet Perry, and Renee M. Bach
Cover design: Renee M. Bach
Series editor: Patricia Lantier-Sampon
Editorial assistants: Mary Dykstra and Diane Laska

Photo credits: Cover and p. 17: © S. K. Patrick/Tom Stack and Associates; pp. 5, 7, 11, 15, and 19: Bob Langrish; p. 9: © Inga Spence/Tom Stack & Associates; p. 13: © Jeff Foott/Tom Stack & Associates; p. 21: © Bob McKeever; p. 22: © Mark Newman/Tom Stack & Associates.

Printed in the United States of America

1 2 3 4 5 6 7 8 9 02 01 00 99 98

Front cover: Mustangs running wild in the sagebrush and snow are the picture of freedom. They can survive on ranges that would be too poor to support most other large animals.

TABLE OF CONTENTS

Words that appear in the glossary are printed in **boldface** type the first time they occur in the text.

EXACTLY WHO GETS CAUGHT?

It is hard to say who gets caught when talking about Mustangs — the horses or the people. Mustangs have captured the imaginations of people since those wild horses first formed their roaming herds.

Some people love Mustangs, and some dislike them. Others just tell stories and legends about the horses. Some of those stories are about as wild as the Mustangs themselves.

One group of stories is about a legendary horse called the Pacing White Mustang.

Mustangs are the so-called "mutts" of the horse world! With a variety of ancestors, they have all kinds of unusual markings and colors.

PACING

Gaits are the different ways horses move along. Pacing is one kind of gait. Other gaits include walking, trotting, and galloping.

Scientists have found fossilized tracks that prove some prehistoric horses knew how to pace. One of these was *Parahipparion*, a horse that lived about three million years ago.

When a horse paces, both legs on one side of its body move forward a step, then the legs on the other side take a step together, and so on. If two people march one behind the other, such as musicians in a parade, their footprints will show a pacing pattern. However, they would never be as swift and smooth as the Pacing White Mustang!

Take a look at the Mustangs in this enclosed area, or paddock. Which of the horses do you think are pacing?

"THE WHITE MUSTANG GLIDED LIKE A GHOST"

More than a hundred years ago in the Old West, news of a magnificent white male Mustang reached a group of people who hunted Mustangs for a living. They decided to look for him.

When he was sighted, a 200-mile (320-km) chase began. The Pacing White Mustang never stopped to eat, drink, or sleep. He left his herd and the hunters far behind. He finally stopped for a long drink. He thought he was free.

But a **vaquero** spotted him, and the Pacing White Mustang was trapped. The vaquero caught him and tied him next to a barrel of water. The Mustang stood still for ten days. When he was sure there would be no escape, he lay down and died.

White Mustangs are rare in the wild, and they stand out. It is difficult for them to hide from predators.

HOW MUSTANGS GOT THEIR FREEDOM

Horses were brought to the New World (North and South America) with European invaders and their African slaves. Some horses, however, became free. Some swam to shore from shipwrecks, some escaped when the invaders fought with American Indians, some got lost, and some just wandered off. These horses turned wild and formed herds of their own.

Those first free horses were mostly from Spanish horse **breeds** called Andalusians and Barbs. In fact, the American word *Mustang* comes from the Spanish word *musteño*, which means "strayed."

Mustangs' coats are all the colors a horse can be: white, cream, yellow, light brown, dark brown, reddish brown or **chestnut**, light red, deep red, gray, and black.

GO WEST, YOUNG HORSE!

The early Mustangs were small, light horses, like the Spanish breeds they came from.

Later, when the new Americans from Europe and Africa moved West, even more varieties of horses became free. Some were draft horses that pulled cannons for the U.S. Army and either broke free or were released. Some were ranchers' horses that had managed to escape.

These large, heavy horses **bred** with the Spanish Mustangs, and many features mixed together in their offspring. This is why some Mustangs may not look as graceful as **domesticated** horses.

Notice how this two-day-old foal's legs are almost as long as its mother's legs. Within hours of being born, foals can run just as fast as the rest of the herd.

HOW ARE MUSTANGS BUILT?

Conformation refers to the way a horse is built. Many Mustangs have a similar conformation. Their hooves are especially hard, and they are sure-footed over rocks and rough ground. Their bellies are tight, and there is usually a slope to their rumps.

Mustangs are small and light compared with other horses, but they can travel great distances, just like the Pacing White Mustang did.

Here's how Mustangs measure up to other horses:

	Mustangs	Other Horses (Averages)
Height	13-15 **hands*** (4 ft. 4 in.-5 ft. or 1.3-1.5 m)	15 hands (5 ft. or 1.5 m)
Weight	700-900 pounds (318-409 kg)	1,000 pounds (454 kg)

* A hand = 4 inches (10.2 cm). Horses' heights are measured to their **withers**.

Mustangs' bodies show more variation than other breeds. Note, in this photograph, how different the various Mustangs are from one another.

ENDANGERED MUSTANGS

When American Indians were forced to move to reservations, many of their horses disappeared, escaped, or were killed by people who did not want them to have this means of transportation.

When Americans began using cars, trucks, and trains for transportation, many horses were freed. By 1930, over eight million Mustangs roamed the Western grasslands. They often lived on land that people wanted for cattle. The horses were hunted down and killed until only a few were left. Some were used for dog food; others just rotted on the land. But a woman named Velma Johnston, from Nevada, thought Mustangs should be treated as endangered wildlife, not as dog food.

Before Mustangs were protected by Congress, they were chased on land and from the air. Sometimes they were captured; often, they were shot.

A WOMAN, A FEW MUSTANGS, LOTS OF KIDS

From 1950 to 1971, Mrs. Johnston, together with hundreds of teachers and thousands of school children, wrote to the U.S. Congress. Johnston was called "Wild Horse Annie" by people who opposed her crusade. Later, people on both sides of the issue referred to her by that name. At last, the "Wild Horse Annie" Bill was passed by Congress to end cruelty to the Mustangs.

Now the government collects as many Mustangs as it can from preserves in Nevada and Colorado. About 70 percent of these Mustangs go up for adoption. The rest go back to the range, where they are provided for and protected. No one is allowed to kill Mustangs anymore.

Free-roaming Mustangs are collected into pens every year. There they are treated for insect pests and diseases.

"MUSTANGS ARE NOTHING BUT TROUBLE!"

Some people think Mustangs are not good riding horses. As one trainer said, "They're nothing but nasty, flea-bitten nags of little use to anyone unless they're looking for trouble." The men who chased the Pacing White Mustang must have felt the same! The Indians, however, valued Mustangs as spiritual brothers. Americans would not have bred Morgans, Rangerbreds, or Quarter Horses without Mustangs.

Mustangs are proud horses that continue to capture the imagination of horse-lovers. The stories and legends that follow this wild breed pay tribute to all these proud horses as well as to the Pacing White Mustang whose ghostly memory haunts America's vast prairies.

Who's there? A week old and wild, this foal could be a champion — with the right trainer.

DIAGRAM AND SCALE OF A HORSE

Here's how to measure a horse with a show of hands.
This beautiful Mustang mare is pictured at full gallop.

Ear
Poll
Crest
Forehead
Mane
Neck
Face
Croup
Hip
Back
Withers
Nostril
Tail
Dock
Cheek
Shoulder
Thigh
Chest
Hock
Gaskin
Barrel
Knee
Elbow
Ankle
Cannon Bone
Hoof

6 ft. (180 cm) — 18 hh
17 hh
16 hh
5 ft. (150 cm) — 15 hh
14 hh
4 ft. (120 cm) — 13 hh
12 hh
11 hh
3 ft. (90 cm) — 10 hh
9 hh
8 hh
2 ft. (60 cm) — 7 hh
6 hh
5 hh
4 hh
1 ft. (30 cm) — 3 hh
2 hh
1 hand

(10-year-old)

1 hand high (hh) = 4 inches (approximately 10 cm)

WHERE TO WRITE OR CALL FOR MORE INFORMATION

National Wild Horse and Burro Program
P.O. Box 12000
Reno, NV 89520-0006
Phone: (702) 785-6583

MORE TO READ AND VIEW

Books (Nonfiction):   *After Columbus: The Horse's Return to America.* V. Herman (Soundprints)

The Complete Guides to Horses and Ponies (series). Jackie Budd (Gareth Stevens)

Great American Horses (series). Victor Gentle and Janet Perry (Gareth Stevens)

Magnificent Horses of the World (series). Tomáš Míček and Dr. Hans-Jörg Schrenk (Gareth Stevens)

Once Upon a Horse: A History of Horses and How They Shaped Our Country. Suzanne Jurmain (Lothrop, Lee & Shepard)

Wild Horses of the Red Desert. Glen Rounds (Holiday House)

Books (Fiction):   *Brumbie Dust.* Reginald Ottley (Harcourt Brace & World)

Saddle Club (series). Bonnie Bryant (Gareth Stevens)

War Pony. Donald Emmet Worcester (Texas Christian Univ. Press)

The White Stallion. Elizabeth Shub (Anthem Books)

Videos (Fiction):   *The Black Stallion.* (MGM Home Video)

Run, Appaloosa, Run. (Walt Disney)

WEB SITES

For the Bureau of Land Management (they control Mustang herds):
  www.blm.gov/whb/

For interactive games:
  www.haynet.net/kidstuff.html

For general horse information:
  www.haynet.net
  www.ladyhawk.mcn.net
  okstate.edu/breeds/horses

Due to the dynamic nature of the Internet, some web sites stay current longer than others. To find additional web sites, use a reliable search engine with one or more of the following keywords to help you locate information about horses: *Andalusians, Barbs, dressage, equitation, Morgans, and ranch.*

GLOSSARY

You can find these words on the pages listed. Reading a word in a sentence helps you understand it even better.

breed (n) — a group of horses that shares the same features as a result of the careful selection of stallions and mares to produce foals 10, 12, 14

breed (v), **bred** — to choose a stallion and a mare with certain features to produce foals with similar features 12

chestnut (CHEST-nut) — a reddish-brown color 10

conformation (KON-for-MAY-shun) — how a horse's body is built 14

croup (KROOP) — the area of the rear of the back that slopes to the tail 22

domesticated (DO-MES-tih-KAY-tid) — tamed enough to live with humans 12

gait — a way of moving. Walking, running, pacing, trotting, and cantering are examples of horses' gaits 6

hand — a unit used to measure horses. It is equal to 4 inches (10.2 cm), about the width of a human hand 14, 22

vaquero (vah-KAIR-oh) — a Mexican cowboy 8

withers (WITH-erz) — the ridge between the shoulder bones of a horse. Horses' heights are measured to the withers 14, 22

INDEX